AXEL M. MOSLER

GREECE PANORAMA

Text by Iris Lemanczyk

EDITIONPANORAMA

GRIECHENLAND

Oh, dieses Licht! Es ist, als leuchten das türkisfarbene Meer, der dunkle Olivenhain, die weiße Klostermauer und auch die sandfarbenen Säulen des Tempels von innen. To Fos – das Licht. Egal, ob pastellfarbene Morgenstimmung auf den Meteorafelsen, das harte, kontrastreiche Mittagslicht auf den Dächern des weiß-blau getünchten Kykladenstädtchens Pyrgos oder ein Sonnenuntergang in allen vorstellbaren Gelb- bis Purpurrotschattierungen im Hafen von Rhodos, das Licht fasziniert nirgendwo mehr als in Griechenland. Es „ist unsäglich scharf und unsäglich mild zugleich. Es bringt die feinste Einzelheit mit einer Deutlichkeit hervor, die das Herz höher schlagen lässt. Es ist mit nichts zu vergleichen als mit Geist", schwärmte der österreichische Dichter Hugo von Hofmannsthal, als er 1908 das griechische Licht sah. To Fos. Das Licht. Land des Lichts und der Sonne. Selbstredend, dass Hellas einen Sonnengott benötigt. Jeden Morgen spannt Helios in seinem östlichen Palast vier Rösser vor den Sonnenwagen und jagt im Galopp übers Firmament, bis der im Westen im Meer versinkt. Dort erfrischt sich Helios, nach den Tagesmühen, mit einem Bad.

Helios' zuverlässige und unermüdliche Ritte sorgen bei Millionen von Touristen jedes Jahr für Urlaubsfreuden und Sonnenbräune. Die meisten Griechen allerdings ziehen schattige Plätze vor. Einer der Lieblingsplätze der Männer ist das Kafenion. Morgens schon trinkt man dort einen Kaffee, überfliegt die Zeitung spielt nebenher mit dem

GREECE

Oh, this light! It is as though the turquoise-coloured sea, the dark olive grove, the white monastery walls and even the sand-coloured pillars of the temple were lit from within. To Fos – the light. Whether the pastel-coloured morning light on the Meteora rocks, the starkly contrasting midday light on the roofs of the blue and whitewashed Cyclades village of Pyrgos or a sunset in all imaginable shades of yellow, red and purple above the harbour of Rhodes, nowhere is the light more fascinating than in Greece. It is "unspeakably sharp and unspeakably mild at the same time. It brings out the finest detail with a clarity that makes the heart beat faster. It can be compared to nothing so much as spirit", enthused the Austrian writer Hugo von Hofmannsthal, when he saw the Grecian light in 1908. To Fos. The light. Land of light and of the sun. It goes without saying that Hellas needs a sun god. Every morning in his palace in the east, Helios harnesses four steeds before the Sun Chariot and gallops across the firmament, before sinking into the western sea, where Helios refreshes himself after the efforts of the day with a bath.

Helios' reliable and tireless ride ensures holiday fun and suntans for the millions of tourists who visit Greece every year. Most Greeks however prefer shady locations. One of the favourite places for men is the coffee shop. Here they drink a cup of coffee in the morning, skim through the newspapers while toying with their worry beads, the rosary-like chain carried in Greece, or stare for a while out of the window. Nothing is happening. Or only apparently nothing,

GRÈCE

Oh, cette lumière ! C'est comme si la mer aux eaux turquoises, les oliveraies brunes, les murs blancs des monastères mais aussi les colonnes beiges des temples rayonnaient de l'intérieur. To Fos – la lumière ! Qu'il s'agisse de la lumière matinale aux tons pastel sur les rochers de Meteora, de la lumière crue et contrastée de midi sur les toits badigeonnés en blanc et bleu de la petite ville de Pyrgos dans les Cyclades ou encore d'un coucher de soleil réunissant tous les tons imaginables du jaune au rouge pourpre dans le port de Rhodes, la lumière n'est nulle part ailleurs aussi fascinante qu'en Grèce. Elle est « à la fois incroyablement crue et incroyablement douce. Elle met en évidence le moindre détail avec une netteté qui fait battre les cœurs plus vite. On ne peut la comparer qu'avec l'esprit », s'extasie Hugo von Hofmannsthal, poète autrichien, lorsqu'il voit la lumière grecque pour la première fois en 1908. To Fos. La lumière. Pays de la lumière et du soleil. Cela va sans dire qu'il faut à Hellas un dieu du soleil. Tous les matins dans son palais oriental, Hélios attelle son char de feu à quatre chevaux et chevauche au galop sur le firmament avant de disparaître à l'ouest dans la mer où il se rafraîchit en prenant un bain après son labeur quotidien.

Les chevauchées fiables et inlassables d'Hélios sont chaque année le garant de vacances réussies et d'un bronzage parfait pour des millions de touristes. Les Grecs préfèrent toutefois en majorité se réfugier à l'ombre. Les hommes, par exemple, fréquentent de préférence le « kafenion » où, dès le matin,

GRECIA

¡Oh, esa luz! Es como si desde su mismo interior refulgieran el mar de color turquesa, el oscuro olivar, el blanco muro del monasterio e incluso las columnas de color arena del templo. "To Fos", la luz. Independientemente de qué nos haya emocionado más: el amanecer de colores pastel sobre las rocas Meteora, la dura luz del mediodía que tanto hace resaltar los contrastes sobre los tejados de la pequeña ciudad de Pyrgos en las islas cicladas o uno de esos ocasos que permiten disfrutar en el puerto de Rodas de todo el espectro imaginable de tonalidades desde el amarillo al púrpura. En ninguna otra parte la luz es tan fascinante como en Grecia. La luz de Grecia es "increíblemente nítida y al mismo tiempo inefablemente suave. Es capaz de sacar a relucir los más insignificantes detalles con una claridad tal, que el corazón empieza a palpitar. No se puede comparar con ninguna otra cosa que no sea el propio espíritu". Con estos elevados tonos se expresaba el poeta austriaco Hugo von Hofmannsthal después de haberse encontrado con la luz griega en 1908. "To Fos". La luz. La tierra de la luz y del sol. Naturalmente que a Hellas, que así llaman a Grecia los propios griegos, no le podía faltar un dios del sol. Cada madrugada el dios Helios unce cuatro corceles a su carro solar en su palacio del oriente para lanzarse al galope por el firmamento. Al final de su carrera, en Occidente, Helios hunde su carro en el mar. Allí se refresca y descansa de los trabajos de la jornada con un buen baño.

GRECIA

Oh, quella luce! È come se si sprigionasse dall'interno del mare turchese, dall'uliveto ombroso e dalle stesse colonne color sabbia del tempio. To Fos – la luce. Quella pastello del cielo del mattino sulle rocce delle meteore, la forte luce madre di contrasti sui tetti del villaggio cicladico tinto in bianco ed azzurro di Pyrgos o tutte le sfumature immaginabili tra il giallo e il rosso porpora di un tramonto nel porto di Rodi. In nessun altro luogo la luce affascina di più che in Grecia. È „indescrivibilmente violenta e al contempo, infinitamente morbida. Quella luce sa scolpire il minimo dettaglio con una chiarezza che fa battere più forte il cuore. Nessun'altra cosa più si avvicina allo spirito", dichiarò appassionatamente il poeta austriaco Hugo von Hofmannsthal descrivendo nel 1908 la luce in Grecia. To Fos. La luce. La terra della luce e del sole. L'Ellade ha dovuto creare una sua divinità del sole, ovviamente. Così, ogni mattino Helios dal suo palazzo ad Oriente attacca al carro del sole quattro destrieri che sprona al galoppo lungo la volta del firmamento. Nel mare d'Occidente, in cui si sprofonda al termine della sua fatica quotidiana, trova refrigerio Helios.

Le perenni ed instancabili cavalcate di Helios assicurano ogni anno a milioni di turisti vacanze piacevoli ed abbronzatura. Quasi tutti i greci però prediligono l'ombra. Uno dei luoghi preferiti dagli uomini è il Kafenion. Al mattino ci si va a prendere un caffè, a sfogliare il giornale ed anche a giocare con il Komboloi, lo scacciapensieri simile ad una

Komboloi, der rosenkranzähnlichen Kette und starrt eine Weile aus dem Fenster oder vor sich hin. Nichts tut sich. Scheinbar nichts, denn im Kafenion werden tagsüber Geschäfte abgewickelt. Man streitet über Politik oder Baugenehmigungen. Der Flaschner nimmt einen Auftrag an, der Postbote legt dort eine Verschnaufpause ein, selbst der Pope schaut vorbei. Abends wird weiter diskutiert, palavert oder die Welt verbessert. Auch fürs Kartenspiel oder Tavli, das griechische Backgammon, finden sich immer begeisterte Mitspieler.

Ein Kafenion gab es im klassischen Griechenland nicht. Zumindest sind sie aus der Zeit des Trojanischen Krieges nicht überliefert. Vielleicht wäre dann alles anders gekommen. Ausgelöst hatte den Krieg angeblich der Streit um die schöne Helena. Weil der Trojaner Paris die Begehrenswerte entführt haben soll, hat ihr Gatte Menelaos mit seinen Verbündeten Troja belagert. Zehn Jahre lang Mord und Totschlag, selbst die Götter mischten mit. So steht es in Homers unsterblichen Versen. Mit ihm, dem Lehrmeister, beginnt die Zeitrechnung des klassischen Griechenlands. Sie fängt 776 v. Chr. mit den Olympischen Spielen an und endet 323 v. Chr. mit dem Tod Alexander des Großen. Eine wichtige Zeit für die westliche Welt, denn Philosophie, Architektur, Medizin und Mathematik gewinnen ihre heute noch gültigen Konturen.

Dabei ist Griechenland nichts weiter als eine Ansammlung aufgesplitterter Kleinstaaten, die meist nur aus einer Stadt, der Polis, und ihrem Hinterland besteht. Jede Polis hütet ihre Unabhängigkeit, mit eigener Armee, eigenem Kalender, eigenen Maßen und Gewichten. Nur die gemeinsame

because business is conducted in the coffee shop throughout the day. People argue about politics or building approvals. The plumber takes on an order, the postman drops in for a short break, and even the local priest calls by. In the evenings, the discussions and conversation continue, and the world is set to rights. Enthusiastic players can always be found for card games or 'tavli', the Greek version of backgammon.

There were no coffee shops in ancient Greece. At least, they have not been handed down since the time of the Trojan War. Perhaps then everything would have been different. Legend has it that the war started over the battle for the beautiful Helen. Because the Trojan Paris is supposed to have abducted the beauty, Menelaus and his allies laid siege to the city of Troy. Ten long years of blood and slaughter followed, with even the Gods becoming involved, or so it is recorded in the immortal verses of Homer. With him, the Master, begins the calendar of Ancient Greece, beginning in 776 BC with the Olympic Games and coming to an end in 323 BC with the death of Alexander the Great. An important time for the Western world, laying the foundations for philosophy, architecture, medicine and mathematics which still apply today.

At the time, Greece was nothing more than a loose confederation of small, divided states, often consisting of only the 'polis' or city-state and its hinterland. Every city-state guarded its own independence, with its own army, own calendar, and own weights and measures, being bound together only by a common language and orthography, the Olympic Games and the Oracle of Delphi. Neverthcless a first step towards an overall Greek identity.

ils boivent un café, jettent un coup d'œil au journal tout en jouant avec leur « komboloi », sorte de chapelet, regardent par la fenêtre ou dans le vide. Il ne se passe rien ici. Du moins en apparence, car le kafenion est un lieu où on traite des affaires pendant la journée. On y discute de politique ou de permis de construire, on y confie un travail au plombier, le facteur y fait une pause pour souffler et même le pope vient faire un petit tour. Le soir, les discussions continuent, on palabre, on refait le monde. On est sûr aussi d'y trouver toujours d'autres joueurs passionnés pour une partie de cartes ou de « tavli », sorte de backgammon grec.

Il n'existait pas de kafenion dans la Grèce classique. Du moins, les récits de la Guerre de Troie n'y font pas allusion et si cela avait été le cas, cela aurait peut-être changé le cours de l'histoire. La guerre aurait été déclenchée suite à l'enlèvement de la belle Hélène, épouse du roi de Sparte, Ménélas, par le troyen Paris. L'époux bafoué assiège alors la ville de Troie avec ses alliés et les dix années qui suivent sont ponctuées par une série de meurtres et d'assassinats, même les Dieux s'en mêlent. Comme le racontent les vers immortels d'Homère. C'est avec lui, le maître, que sonne l'avènement de la Grèce classique. Elle commence en 776 avant Jésus-Christ avec les Jeux Olympiques et s'achève en l'an 323 avant notre ère avec la mort d'Alexandre le Grand. Une période capitale pour le monde occidental, car elle voit naître les bases, encore valables aujourd'hui, de la philosophie, de l'architecture, de la médecine et des mathématiques.

Pourtant, la Grèce n'est rien d'autre que le regroupement de plusieurs petits états éclatés constitués pour la plupart d'une ville, la polis, et d'un domaine rural alentours. Chaque

Las incansables y puntuales cabalgadas de Helios hacen posible que año tras año millones de turistas puedan disfrutar en Grecia de unas vacaciones de ensueño y broncearse al sol. La mayoría de los griegos prefiere pasar las horas más soleadas a la sombra. Uno de los refugios preferidos de los hombres es el "kafenion". Ya bien de mañana los hombres disfrutan allí del primer café mientras le echan una ojeada al periódico y juegan distraídamente con el "komboloi", una cadena similar por su forma a un rosario. Está claro que el kafenion es el lugar ideal para reflexionar un rato de vez en cuando con la mirada perdida más allá de la ventana. La vida parece detenida, pero es sólo una impresión, porque en el kafenion se apalabran los negocios durante el día. Mientras se discute sobre política o licencias de construcción, el fontanero consigue un encargo, el cartero hace una pausa... Hasta el pope (el sacerdote ortodoxo) pasa por allí. Por la noche se sigue discutiendo, charlando o mejorando el mundo. Y siempre se encuentra a alguien con muchas ganas de jugar a las cartas o al "tavli", el backgammon griego.

En la Grecia clásica no había nada como el kafenion. Al menos no está documentada su existencia en la época de la Guerra de Troya. Quizás la historia hubiera tomado entonces otro camino. La leyenda dice que una disputa en torno a la hermosa Helena desencadenó la guerra. Al parecer el troyano Paris secuestró a la bella y por eso el marido de ésta, Menelaos, puso sitio a Troya junto a sus aliados. Siguieron diez años de asesinatos y enfrentamientos durante los cuales hasta los dioses tomaron partido. Así consta en los inmortales versos de Homero. Con él, maestro, comienza la época

corona del rosario. Lo sguardo resta fisso, per un attimo, davanti a quello che accade fuori dalla finestra oppure davanti a sé. L'immobilità è totale, ma solo in apparenza. Infatti al Kafenion ogni giorno si concludono affari. Si discute di politica o di concessioni edilizie. L'idraulico trova un lavoro da fare, il postino fa una sosta per riposarsi, anche il pope viene a dare un'occhiata. Di sera si portano avanti discussioni, ci si dilunga in chiacchiere o si costruisce un mondo migliore. Anche per le carte o il tavli, il backgammon greco, si trovano sempre entusiasti compagni di gioco.

Nella Grecia classica il Kafenion non c'era, o almeno quest'istituzione non ci è stata tramandata dalla guerra di Troia. Se così fosse stato, forse le cose sarebbero andate in modo completamente diverso. Si dice che la guerra fu scatenata per la contesa della bella Elena. Il troiano Paride avrebbe rapito l'amata inducendo il consorte Menelao con i suoi alleati all'assedio di Troia. Dieci anni di stragi ed omicidi in una vicenda che chiamò l'intervento addirittura degli dei, come declama Omero nei suoi versi immortali. Con lui, il Maestro, si apre il periodo della Grecia classica, dai giochi olimpici del 776 a. C. alla morte di Alessandro il Grande nel 323 a. C.: una fase importante per l'Occidente che su quella cultura ha modellato i suoi fondamenti, oggi ancora validi, nella filosofia, nell'architettura, nella medicina e nella matematica.

La Grecia dell'epoca è costituita da numerosi staterelli frammentati, quasi tutti formati soltanto da una città, la polis, e il suo entroterra. Ogni polis difende la propria indipendenza con un suo esercito, un suo calendario, pesi e

Sprache und Schrift sowie die Olympischen Spiele und das Orakel von Delphi verbinden sie. Immerhin, ein erster Schritt zur gesamtgriechischen Identität.
In Olympia, der wunderschön gelegenen kleinen Siedlung, in der damals nur einige Bauern, Hirten und Priester lebten, kämpften die Athleten zu Ehren des Gottes Zeus. Zuerst nur im Stadionlauf, später kamen dann Ring- und Fünfkampf hinzu. Die fünf Disziplinen waren: Laufen, Weitsprung, Speerwurf, Diskus und Ringen. Der „Olympische Geist" und „Dabeisein ist alles" sind allerdings Erfindungen der Neuzeit. Das Motto hieß: Siegen um jeden Preis. Neben dem Lorbeerkranz erhielt der Sieger von seiner stolzen Heimat ein üppiges Salär. Grund genug, die Schiedsrichter nach allen Regeln der Kunst zu bestechen und zu dopen, was das Zeug hielt. Olympia zog die Massen an. Was nicht nur an den Wettkämpfen gelegen haben soll, sondern auch am Olympischen Orakel. Aus der Opferasche des Zeus-Altars deuteten dort Seher die Zukunft.
Voraussagen waren im klassischen Griechenland von großer Bedeutung. Viele Herrscher der Stadtstaaten wandten sich an das Orakel von Delphi, um Entscheidungen über Kriege zu treffen, oder um den geeigneten Zeitpunkt zu erfragen, um in der Fremde neue Handelsstützpunkte zu gründen. Als Medium des Orakels diente eine Priesterin, die Pythia. Sie fiel in Trance, vermutlich durch halluzinogene Substanzen und weissagte im Innern des Tempels. Prophetes, also Sprecher, verkündeten dann den Herrschern und Ratsuchenden die Worte der Pythia. Das Orakel von Delphi wurde dadurch zur Informationsbörse für die griechische Welt schlechthin.

In Olympia, the amazingly beautiful tiny settlement populated at the time by only a few farmers, shepherds and priests, the athletes competed with each other in honour of the god Zeus. First only in races in the stadium, followed later by wrestling and the pentathlon. The five disciplines were running, long jump, javelin throwing, the discus and wrestling. The "Olympics spirit" and "Playing the game" however are inventions of modern times. The motto of the time was "Victory at any price". In addition to the laurel wreath, the victor received from his proud home state a generous salary, more than enough reason to bribe the umpires as far as possible and use performance-enhancing drugs. Olympia attracted the masses. This was supposed to have been due not only to the competitions, but also to the Olympic Oracle, where seers foretold the future on the altar of Zeus from the ashes of sacrificial offerings.
Prophesies were of great importance in ancient Greece. Many rulers of city-states turned to the Oracle of Delphi, before making decisions about wars, or to ask about the right time for establishing new trading centres abroad. The medium of the Oracle was a priestess, the Pythia. She fell into a trance, probably induced by hallucinogenic substances and made her prophecies in the inner sanctum of the temple. Prophets, i.e. speakers, then proclaimed the words of the Pythia to the rulers or others seeking advice. The Oracle of Delphi thus became a source of information for the Greek world as such.
Over the course of time, two city-states assumed a leading role amongst the 'polis': Sparta and Athens. Sparta devoted itself to military skills, while Athens concentrated on the

polis cultive son indépendance avec sa propre armée, son propre calendrier, ses propres unités de poids et de mesures. Ces cités-états n'ont en commun que la langue, l'écriture ainsi que les Jeux Olympiques et l'Oracle de Delphes. Ce qui constitue, tout de même, une première étape vers une identité grecque.

A Olympie, petit village merveilleusement situé où ne vivaient autrefois que quelques paysans, bergers et prêtres, les athlètes se battaient en l'honneur du dieu Zeus. D'abord seulement à la course de stade, plus tard dans des combats de lutte et au pentathlon. Les cinq disciplines dans lesquelles ils devaient concourir étaient la course, le saut en longueur, le lancer du javelot, le lancer du disque et la lutte. L'« esprit olympique », « l'essentiel, c'est de participer » sont toutefois des inventions des temps modernes. La devise à l'époque était : « Gagner à tout prix ». Outre une couronne de lauriers, le vainqueur se voyait remettre un salaire rondelet par sa patrie d'origine, fière de lui, ce qui constituait une raison suffisante pour corrompre les arbitres et se doper tant et plus. Olympie attirait les foules, non seulement en raison des compétitions qui s'y déroulaient mais aussi à cause de l'oracle d'Olympie où des devins lisaient l'avenir dans les cendres des victimes sacrifiées sur l'autel de Zeus.

Les prédictions jouaient un grand rôle dans la Grèce classique. De nombreux monarques de ces cités-états consultaient l'Oracle de Delphes avant de prendre des décisions concernant les guerres ou pour connaître la meilleure date pour fonder un nouveau comptoir commercial à l'étranger. Une prêtresse, la pythie, servait de médium à l'oracle. Elle tombait dans un état de transe, provoqué probablement par des substances

de la Grecia clásica que empieza en 776 a. de C. con los juegos olímpicos y termina en 323 a. de C. con la muerte de Alejandro Magno. Se trata sin duda de un período clave para el mundo occidental, ya que la filosofía, la arquitectura, la medicina y las matemáticas asentaron sus principios todavía vigentes en aquel lejano pasado.

Y eso que Grecia no era más que un conjunto de pequeños estados independientes que, por regla general, se limitaban a una sola ciudad, la Polis, y su entorno rural. Cada Polis mantenía un ejército propio para custodiar su independencia, seguía su propio calendario y tenía su propio sistema de pesos y medidas. Sólo el idioma y la escritura comunes, los juegos olímpicos y el oráculo de Delfi unían a todos los helenos. Pero esos elementos supusieron el primer paso hacia una identidad panhelena.

En Olimpia, una pequeña colonia con una bellísima localización, donde, en aquel entonces, no residían más que algunos campesinos, pastores y sacerdotes, empezaron a competir los atletas a mayor gloria de Zeus. Al principio la única competición era la carrera en el estadio. Más tarde se fueron uniendo otras disciplinas como la lucha libre y el pentatlón. Las cinco disciplinas eran: la carrera, el salto, el lanzamiento de jabalina, el lanzamiento del disco y la lucha libre. En cambio el "espíritu olímpico" y el famoso lema de "lo importante es participar" son inventos de la era moderna. En aquel entonces lo importante era ganar a cualquier precio. Además de la corona de laurel el ganador recibía un pingüe premio en metálico pagado por su orgullosa patria. Alicientes más que suficientes no sólo para sobornar a los árbitros por todos los medios disponibles, sino también para

misure diverse. Il solo denominatore comune è la lingua e la scrittura, oltre ai giochi olimpici e all'oracolo di Delfi, ed è comunque un primo passo verso l'identità panellenica.

Ad Olimpia, un piccolo centro posto in una splendida località in cui all'epoca vivevano solo pochi contadini, pastori e sacerdoti, gli atleti si cimentavano in competizioni in onore del dio Zeus. In un primo tempo si tenevano solo gare di corsa, a cui si aggiunsero successivamente le competizioni nella lotta e nel pentathlon. Le cinque discipline erano la corsa, il salto in lungo, il lancio del giavellotto, il lancio del disco e la lotta. Lo „spirito olimpico" e „l'essere presenti è tutto" sono comunque acquisizioni di tempi più recenti. Ad Olimpia vigeva un solo imperativo: "vincere a qualsiasi costo". Oltre alla corona d'alloro il vincitore riceveva dalla sua orgogliosa patria un cospicuo compenso: quanto bastava per corrompere a regola d'arte i giudici e doparsi abbondantemente. Olimpia attirava le masse e non solo per via dei giochi ma anche per l'oracolo che in quella città risiedeva. Dalla cenere delle vittime sacrificali i veggenti leggevano il futuro sull'altare del luogo, dedicato a Zeus.

Le profezie rivestivano un ruolo particolarmente significativo nella Grecia classica. Molti regnanti delle città-stato consultavano l'oracolo di Delfi prima di prendere decisioni sulle guerre, per sapere quando il momento era propizio per intervenire o per fondare nuovi punti d'appoggio commerciali in territori stranieri. La medium dell'oracolo era una sacerdotessa detta pizia, che, dopo essere caduta in trance probabilmente sotto l'effetto di sostanze allucinogene, vaticinava all'interno del tempio. I profeti, cioè gli an-

Mit der Zeit übernahmen zwei Städte eine Führungsrolle unter den Polis: Sparta und Athen. Sparta verschrieb sich dem Kämpfen, während Athen auf die Verbreitung demokratischer Strukturen aus war und die schönen Künste vorantrieb. Athen – das sind heute eigentlich zwei Städte. Die eine, eine junge Millionen-Stadt, hektisch, mit täglichem Verkehrschaos und dem beißenden, kaum erträglichen to Néfos – dem Smog. Die andere, das antike Athen, ist ein Wallfahrtsort für Kunstliebhaber, der sich durch Schwefeldioxid allmählich zu bröseligem Gips verwandelt. Was wäre Athen ohne die Akropolis? Was ohne den Parthenon, das einzigartige Marmor-Wunderwerk? Mitten in der Stadt erhebt sich der kahle Kalkfelsen der Akropolis mit dem Heiligtum der städtischen Schutzgöttin Athene, zu deren Ehren der prächtige Parthenon-Tempel gebaut wurde.
Von hier oben erkennt man die Berge von Pentéli. In seinen riesigen Steinbrüchen wird heute noch Marmor abgebaut. Vor 2500 Jahren trieben dort Sklaven Holzpflöcke ins Gestein, die sie wässerten. Das Holz quoll auf, sprengte den Stein, der dann über mehr als 15 Kilometer bis zur Akropolis gezogen werden musste, bevor er hier zum Parthenon heranwuchs, diesem ersten von den Stufen bis zum Dach ganz aus Marmor hergestellten Tempel.
Von hier oben blickt man auch auf ein unüberschaubares Häusermeer. Doch die Athener haben keine Probleme mit dem Häusermeer, denn für sie zählt in erster Linie ihr Jitoniá. Ihr Viertel, in dem fast jeder jeden kennt. Manchmal umfasst es nur zwei Häuserblocks. Der Gemüsehändler, Arzt, Advokat, auch der Fischhändler sind in unmittelbarer

spreading of democratic structures and promoted the fine arts. The Athens of today is actually two cities. The one, a young city of millions, hectic, with daily traffic chaos and the choking, almost unbearable 'to Néfos' – the smog. The other, the ancient Athens, is a place of pilgrimage for art-lovers, which due to the action of sulphur dioxide is being gradually converted into crumbling plaster. What would Athens be without the Acropolis? What would it be without the Parthenon, this unique wonder of marble? In the centre of the city rises the barren limestone outcrop of the Acropolis, the 'high city' with the sanctuary of the city's protecting goddess Athene, in whose honour the magnificent Parthenon Temple was constructed.
From up here one can see the mountains of Pentéli, in whose huge quarries marble is still quarried today. 2,500 years ago, slaves cut out the blocks by driving wooden wedges into the stone, which they then watered. The wood swelled, gradually cleaving the rock, which then had to be drawn more than 15 kilometres to the Acropolis, before becoming part of the Parthenon, this first temple being built from the steps to the roof entirely of marble.
From here one looks out over an undulating sea of houses. Yet the Athenians have no problems with this sea of houses, because it is their 'Jitoniá' which counts above all. Their district, in which almost everyone knows everybody else. Sometimes this may be made up of no more than two blocks of houses. The grocer, doctor, lawyer, the fishmonger, all live right next to each other. In the backyards flourish piquant oregano and rosemary, deep red bougainvillea and delicate pink oleander in rusty metal tins or black plastic

hallucinogènes, et prophétisait à l'intérieur du temple. Des prophètes, des porte-parole donc, rapportaient ensuite les mots de la pythie aux monarques et à ceux venus pour chercher conseil. C'est ainsi que l'Oracle de Delphes devient ainsi la bourse d'information du monde grec.

Au fil du temps, deux cités se détachent de toutes ces polis : Sparte et Athènes. Tandis que Sparte se voue aux combats, Athènes se consacre à la diffusion des structures démocratiques et s'efforce de promouvoir les beaux-arts. Athènes – ce sont aujourd'hui deux villes en fait. La première est une ville jeune de plusieurs millions d'habitants, trépidante, avec des embouteillages quotidiens et le « nefos », ce nuage de pollution mordant et presque insupportable. L'autre, l'Athènes antique, est un lieu de pèlerinage pour les amateurs d'art où, peu à peu, les bâtiments et les monuments subissent les dégradations dues à l'anhydride sulfureux qui transforme les ciments et les plâtres en une substance friable. Que serait Athènes sans l'Acropole ? Sans le Parthénon, cette œuvre d'art extraordinaire en marbre ? Le rocher calcaire nu de l'Acropole se dresse en plein cœur de la ville avec le sanctuaire de la patronne de la ville, Athéna, en l'honneur de laquelle le temple du Parthénon a été édifié.

D'ici en haut, on aperçoit la montagne de Pentélique qui abrite d'immenses carrières dont on extrait encore aujourd'hui du marbre blanc. Les esclaves qui y travaillaient il y a 2 500 ans, enfonçaient des piquets en bois dans la roche puis versaient de l'eau dessus. Le bois gonflait, faisant éclater la roche qu'il fallait ensuite tirer sur plus de 15 kilomètres jusqu'à l'Acropole pour y construire le Parthénon, le premier temple entièrement en marbre de la première marche au toit.

doparse con todo lo que estaba disponible en aquella época. Los juegos olímpicos atraían a las masas. Pero el tremendo atractivo del evento no sólo se debía a las competiciones, sino también al oráculo olímpico. Basándose en las cenizas de las ofrendas que se realizaban sobre el altar local de Zeus, los adivinos vaticinaban el futuro.

En toda la Grecia clásica las predicciones tenían una gran importancia. Muchos soberanos de las polis se dirigían al oráculo de Delfi para tomar decisiones sobre las guerras o para preguntar a los dioses cuál era el mejor momento para establecer nuevos emporios comerciales en tierras forasteras. El médium del oráculo era normalmente una sacerdotisa, la pitia, que caía en trance, probablemente bajo los efectos de sustancias alucinógenas y hacía predicciones en el interior del templo. Los profetas, los "portavoces" de los dioses, anunciaban a continuación a los soberanos e interesados las palabras de la pitia. De esta forma el oráculo de Delfi se convirtió en la bolsa de informaciones por excelencia para el mundo heleno.

Con el tiempo dos ciudades alcanzaron el liderazgo entre las polis: Esparta y Atenas. Esparta era una polis de vocación guerrera mientras que Atenas se dedicó más bien a la difusión de sus estructuras democráticas así como al fomento de las bellas artes. Atenas en realidad hoy abarca dos ciudades. La primera es una joven metrópoli de millones de habitantes, estresada y sumida en un caos cotidiano de tráfico así como en una asfixiante, casi insoportable, contaminación atmosférica. Para los locales: "to Néfos". La otra, la antigua Atenas, es un lugar de peregrinación para los amantes del arte que el anhídrido

nunciatori delle profezie, comunicavano quindi ai regnanti e a chi cercava consigli le sentenze della pizia. L'oracolo di Delfi divenne in questo modo il miglior centro d'informazione del mondo greco.

Nel tempo due città assunsero il ruolo di guida tra le polis: Sparta e Atene. Sparta si dedicò ai combattimenti mentre Atene appoggiò la diffusione di organizzazioni democratiche e favorì lo sviluppo delle belle arti. Atene oggi ha due anime. Da una lato c'è la città giovane di milioni d'abitanti, frenetica, immersa nel caos del traffico quotidiano e in un Néfos, lo smog, pungente e quasi insopportabile. L'altra, l'antica Atene, il luogo di pellegrinaggio degli amanti dell'arte, si sta lentamente trasformando in gesso friabile per gli effetti del biossido di zolfo. Ma cosa sarebbe Atene senza l'Acropoli? Cosa sarebbe senza il Partenone, il meraviglioso tempio in marmo unico al mondo? Al centro della città si erge la nuda rupe calcarea dell'Acropoli con il luogo sacro della dea protettrice della città di Atene in onore della quale fu eretto lo splendido Partenone.

Da questo punto si delineano in alto i monti Penteli dalle cui enormi cave di pietra si estrae ancor oggi il marmo. 2500 anni fa gli schiavi piantavano picchetti in legno nella roccia che bagnavano con acqua. Il legno, dilatandosi, spaccava la pietra che da qui doveva essere trascinata per oltre 15 chilometri fino all'acropoli. Così fu eretto il Partenone, il primo tempio costruito interamente in marmo dai gradini al tetto.

Da quest'altura lo sguardo abbraccia un mare sterminato di costruzioni, ma l'intensa urbanizzazione non disturba gli ateniesi. Ciò che a loro in fondo interessa è il loro Jito-

Nähe. In den Hinterhöfen gedeihen würziger Oregano, und Rosmarin, tiefrote Bougainvillea und zartrosa Oleander in rostigen Blechkanistern oder schwarzen Plastikkübeln. Im Nachbarhaus gibt es ein Periptero, einen winzigen Kiosk mit Zeitschriften, Zigaretten, Kämmen, Kondomen, Keksen und mit allen Geheimnissen und Skandälchen des Viertels, die der Inhaber des Periptero gerne preisgibt.

Griechenland hat schon viele Eroberer kommen und gehen sehen. „Sie haben alle nur genommen und auf unsere Kosten gelebt", philosophiert Jannis Daskalos. „Die Eroberer von heute sind da anders: Sie geben ihr Geld bei uns aus und verschwinden nach kurzer Zeit wieder freiwillig." Rund 35 Prozent des griechischen Wirtschaftsvolumens macht das Geschäft mit dem Tourismus aus. Seit Anfang der 1990er Jahre besuchen mehr Touristen das Land, als es Einwohner hat. Und das sind fast elf Millionen. Flugzeuge und Fähren bringen die Urlauber auf fast jede Insel, an fast jeden Strand. Griechenland galt schon 1888 als, für damalige Verhältnisse, einfach zu bereisen. Im Baedeker Reiseführer stand damals: „Eine Reise nach Griechenland gehört auch für uns Deutsche nicht mehr zu jenen außerordentlichen Glücksfällen des Lebens, welche nur Einzelnen zu Theil wird. In 14 Stunden bringt der Dampfer den Reisenden von Brindisi nach Corfu und von da in weiteren 16 Stunden nach Patras, wo er die 1887 eröffnete Eisenbahn erreicht, welche ihn in 4,5 Stunden nach Korinth, in 9 Stunden nach Athen befördert (von Brindisi nach Athen im ganzen 35 Stunden)." Wie lange man von Köln, Hamburg oder München nach Brindisi brauchte, verschweigt der Reiseführer allerdings.

tubs. In the neighbouring house is a 'periptero', a tiny kiosk selling magazines, cigarettes, combs, condoms, biscuits, and all the secrets and petty scandals of the quarter, which the owner of the periptero is happy to reveal.

Greece has seen many conquerors come and go. "They all simply took, and lived at our expense", philosophises Jannis Daskalos. "The conquerors of today are different: they spend their money here with us, and then go home voluntarily a while later." The tourist business makes up around 35% of the Greek economy. Since the beginning of the 1990's, the tourists visiting the country every year even outnumber the population, and that is almost 11 million. Aircraft and ferries take the holiday-makers to almost every island, almost every beach. Even in 1888, with the transport facilities of the time, Greece was considered an easy destination to tour. The Baedecker travel guide of the time reported: "A trip to Greece is now for we Germans too no longer one of those unusually fortunate events in life which can only be enjoyed by the few. In 14 hours, the steamer can carry the traveller from Brindisi to Corfu, and from there in a further 16 hours to Patras, where he can take the railway, opened in 1887, which brings him in 4.5 hours to Corinth, and in 9 hours to Athens (from Brindisi to Athens in a total of 35 hours)." The guide neglects to say however how long it took to get to Brindisi from Cologne, Hamburg or Munich.

Jannis Daskalos lives on Leros, one of around 3,050 Greek islands, of which however only 167 are inhabited. Jannis is actually a fisherman. But only in winter does he set out regularly in his boat. In winter, when his wife Eleni then

La Grèce a déjà vu passer de nombreux conquérants. « Tous autant qu'ils étaient, ils n'ont fait que prendre et ont vécu à nos frais », philosophe Jannis Daskalos. « Les conquérants modernes sont différents : ils dépensent leur argent chez nous et disparaissent rapidement de leur plein gré ». Environ 35 % du volume économique de la Grèce proviennent du tourisme. Depuis le début des années 1990, le nombre de touristes est supérieur au nombre d'habitants. Et il y en a presque onze millions. Les avions et les ferrys conduisent les touristes dans presque n'importe quelle île, sur presque n'importe quelle plage. La Grèce, dès 1888, était considérée comme un pays dans lequel il était facile de circuler en ce temps-là. Dans le guide de voyage allemand Baedecker, on pouvait lire à l'époque : « Un voyage en Grèce n'est plus pour nous, Allemands, le produit d'un hasard extraordinaire accordé seulement à quelques élus. En 14 heures, le bateau à vapeur amène les voyageurs de Brindisi à Corfou puis, en 16 heures, jusqu'à Patras où ils rejoignent la ligne ferroviaire inaugurée en 1887 et qui les conduit en 4 heures et demie à Corinthe, en 9 heures à Athènes (35 heures en tout de Brindisi à Athènes). » Le guide ne précise pas toutefois combien de temps il faut pour rallier Brindisi depuis Cologne, Hambourg ou Munich.

Jannis Daskalos vit à Leros, l'une des 3 050 îles grecques environ dont 167 seulement sont habitées. Jannis est pêcheur de son état en temps normal, mais il ne sort plus régulièrement en mer qu'en hiver. En hiver, sa femme Eleni trouve également le temps de discuter longuement avec ses voisines, ce qui est presque impossible en été, car tous deux travaillent jusqu'à 20 heures par jour. Jannis n'est alors

sulfuroso va convirtiendo en una especie de yeso que se desmigaja al tacto. ¿Pero qué sería Atenas sin la Acrópolis? ¿Qué sería Atenas sin el Partenón, esa singularísima maravilla de mármol? En medio de la ciudad se eleva el monte pelado de roca calina que sirve de base a la Acrópolis. Allí se encuentra el santuario de la diosa protectora de la ciudad, Atenea. En su honor se erigió en la época clásica el suntuoso templo del Partenón.

Grecia ya ha visto a muchos invasores venir e irse. "Todos ellos se dedicaron a llevarse lo que pudieron y a vivir a nuestra costa" filosofea Jannis Daskalos. "Los invasores de hoy son diferentes: primero se gastan aquí su dinero y poco después se van voluntariamente". El negocio del turismo es responsable de en torno al 35 por ciento del volumen económico griego. Desde principios de los años 90 el país recibe más turistas que habitantes tiene. Y son casi once millones. Prácticamente todas las islas y todas las playas se pueden alcanzar en avión o en barco. Ya en 1888 se consideraba que Grecia era un país relativamente fácil de recorrer. En la guía de turistas de Baedeck ya se podía leer entonces: "Para nosotros los alemanes un viaje a Grecia ya no es el producto de uno de esos extraordinarios golpes de suerte de la vida que sólo muy pocos consiguen disfrutar. En tan sólo 14 horas el barco a vapor traslada al viajero de Brindisi a Corfú y desde allí en otras 16 horas a Patras, donde se puede alcanzar la terminal de la línea de ferrocarril que se inauguró en 1887. En el tren se puede alcanzar Corinto en 4,5 horas, en 9 horas Atenas (por tanto de Brindisi a Atenas en 35 horas)". Lo que no dice la guía es cuánto se tardaba desde Colonia, Hamburgo o Múnich hasta Brindisi.

niá, il quartiere in cui ci si conosce quasi tutti, uno spazio vitale che a volte comprende soltanto due isolati. Il fruttivendolo, il medico, l'avvocato e il pescivendolo: tutti vivono o esercitano lì, tutti sono a un tiro di schioppo. Nei cortili interni, in latte arrugginite o secchi di plastica nera crescono vigorose piante d'aromatico origano e rosmarino, bouganvillee rosso acceso ed oleandri rosa pallido. Nella casa del vicino c'è un periptero, un minuscolo chiosco in cui si vendono riviste, sigarette, pettini, profilattici, biscotti e tutti i segreti e i piccoli scandali del quartiere, che il proprietario del periptero è lieto di raccontare.

La Grecia ha già visto andare e venire molti conquistatori. „Tutti ci hanno solo derubato e hanno vissuto sulle nostre spalle", commenta filosofico Jannis Daskalos. „I conquistatori di oggi però sono diversi: spendono da noi il loro denaro, restano poco e se ne vanno presto senza bisogno di cacciarli." Il turismo è una ricchezza che rappresenta circa il 35 per cento del reddito nazionale. Dall'inizio degli anni novanta la presenza di turisti in Grecia è superiore al numero degli abitanti: quasi undici milioni sono i vacanzieri che sbarcano da aerei e traghetti su quasi tutte le isole e su quasi tutte le spiagge. Già dal 1888 la Grecia si presentava come un paese facilmente visitabile per le condizioni della fine Ottocento. Così recitava all'epoca la guida turistica Baedecker: „Anche per noi tedeschi un viaggio in Grecia non è più l'evento straordinario che può accadere nella vita di pochi fortunati. In quattordici ore il piroscafo trasporta i viaggiatori da Brindisi a Corfù. In altre sedici attracca a Patrasso per raggiungere la ferrovia inaugurata nel 1887. Di lì in quattro ore e mezzo si arriva

Jannis Daskalos lebt auf Leros, einer der rund 3050 griechischen Inseln, von denen allerdings nur 167 bewohnt sind. Eigentlich ist Jannis Fischer. Aber nur noch im Winter fährt er häufiger mit dem Boot hinaus. Im Winter, wenn seine Frau Eleni auch mal Zeit für einen ausgiebigen Tratsch mit ihren Nachbarinnen findet. Das ist im Sommer kaum möglich, da sind alle fast 20 Stunden am Tag vollauf beschäftigt. Dann ist Jannis ab und zu mal Fischer, meistens aber Pensionsbesitzer, Einkäufer, Kellner und Barkeeper. Eleni mutiert ab Mai von der Hausfrau zur Köchin, Wasch- und Putzfrau, Buchhalterin sowie Empfangsdame. Sobald die Touristen kommen, verändert sich das Leben auf Leros völlig. Tagsüber zollen die Fremden aus England, Deutschland, aus Holland, Dänemark oder Polen den herrlichen Stränden, Helios und dem Meer Tribut. Dem Meer mit seinem einzigartigen Türkis, von dem der deutsche Schriftsteller Kasimir Edschmid 1932 schrieb: „Diese Meerfarbe ist vielleicht der einzige antike Zauber, den die Welt noch hat. Das ganze Drama unserer Weltgeschichte hat sich hier abgespielt, es hat Imperien erhoben und hat Imperien versenkt mit einer tragischen Laune und Farbigkeit, wie sie nur die Dramatik des Mittelmeers kennt. Man braucht das Meer nur zu riechen. Es duftet nach schönen und heroischen Göttern."

Die Götter finden die Heroen von heute vielleicht beim Erklimmen des Felsen zur Burg Brouzi, oder beim Besichtigen der Klöster und Kirchen auf der 53 Quadratkilometer großen Insel. Beliebt sind auch Mopedtouren, um die Insel zu erkunden. In den lauen Sommernächten gibt es in den Tavernen von Agia Marina oder Platanos

has time for a long gossip with her neighbours. This is almost impossible in the summer, because then everybody is rushed off their feet for almost 20 hours per day. Then Jannis is only a part-time fisherman, but for most of the time a guesthouse-keeper, buyer, waiter and barkeeper. Eleni changes from May from a housewife into a cook, washerwoman, cleaner, bookkeeper and receptionist. As soon as the tourists arrive, life on Leros changes completely. Every day the foreigners from England, Germany, Holland, Denmark and Poland arrive to pay tribute to the beautiful beaches, the sun and the sea. The sea with its unique vibrant turquoise colour, of which the German author Kasimir Edschmid wrote in 1932: "This sea colour is perhaps the only ancient magic which still exists in the world today. The whole drama of our world history has been played out here, empires have risen and empires have fallen in a welter of tragedy and colour known only in the dramatic setting of the Mediterranean. One only needs to smell the sea. It is sweet with the scent of beautiful and heroic gods."

The heroes of today can perhaps encounter the gods by climbing the rock up to the fortress of Brouzi, or by visiting the cloisters and churches on this island of only 53 sq. km. Moped tours are another popular way of exploring the island. In the warm summer evenings, the taverns of Agia Marina or Platanos are full to bursting point. Greek wine flows in torrents, music sounds out from the loudspeakers. Again and again the same melody with bouzoukis, synthesizers and percussion. Again and again the sirtaki. The foreigners love it. The whole world thinks that the sirtaki, as danced by Alexis Zorba in the film "Zorba the

pêcheur qu'occasionnellement, la plupart du temps, il est directeur de pension, serveur, barman et fait également les courses. Eleni, femme au foyer normalement, se transforme quant à elle dès le mois de mai en cuisinière, blanchisseuse et femme de ménage, comptable et réceptionniste. Dès que les touristes arrivent, la vie change du tout au tout à Leros. Pendant la journée, les étrangers venant d'Angleterre, d'Allemagne, de Hollande, du Danemark ou de Pologne profitent des plages magnifiques, du soleil et de la mer. La mer avec ses magnifiques eaux turquoises à propos de laquelle l'écrivain allemand, Kasimir Edschmid, a écrit en 1932 : « La couleur de la mer est peut-être le seul charme antique encore existant au monde. Tout le drame de notre histoire universelle s'est déroulé ici, elle a conquis des empires et en a englouti d'autres avec une humeur tragique et des couleurs que seule la Méditerranée connaît dans ses moments dramatiques. Il suffit de sentir la mer pour ressentir la présence proche des Dieux, beaux et héroïques. »

Peut-être que les héros d'aujourd'hui rencontrent les Dieux dans l'ascension du rocher vers la forteresse de Brouzi, ou lors de la visite des monastères et des églises sur cette île de 53 kilomètres carrés. Les excursions à mobylette sont également un moyen idéal de partir à la découverte de l'île. Au cours des tièdes nuits d'été, impossible de trouver une chaise libre dans les tavernes d'Agia Marina ou de Platanos. Le vin grec coule à flots tandis que les haut-parleurs déversent de la musique. Toujours la même mélodie avec bouzouki, synthétiseur et percussions. Encore et toujours le sirtaki. Les étrangers l'adorent. Le monde entier croit que le sirtaki, tel qu'il est dansé par Alexis Zorba dans le film

Jannis Daskalos reside en Leros, una de las cerca de 3050 islas griegas, de las cuales, por cierto, sólo están habitadas 167. En realidad Jannis es pescador. Pero ahora casi sólo sale con el barco en invierno. En invierno, que es la época en que su mujer Eleni puede encontrar tiempo para una buena charla con sus vecinas. En verano eso es prácticamente imposible, ya que durante la estación alta todos están ocupados casi 20 horas al día. Entonces Jannis sólo es pescador ocasionalmente, ya que la mayor parte del tiempo se dedica a regentar su pensión, a hacer las compras y a trabajar de camarero y barman. A partir de mayo Eleni pasa de ser ama de casa a ser cocinera, lavandera, limpiadora, contable y recepcionista. Tan pronto los turistas empiezan a llegar, la vida de Leros se transforma completamente. Durante el día los forasteros procedentes de Inglaterra, Alemania, Holanda, Dinamarca o Polonia rinden su tributo a las fantásticas playas, a Helios y al mar. A ese mar con su inigualable color turquesa del que el escritor alemán Kasimir Edschmid escribió en 1932: "Este color del mar es quizás el único hechizo antiguo que le queda al mundo. Todo el dramatismo de nuestra historia universal ha tenido lugar aquí, ha visto elevarse imperios para derrumbarse más tarde manteniendo siempre esa tonalidad y ambiente trágicos del mar que sólo el alma dramática del Mediterráneo posee. Tan sólo hace falta olerlo. Este mar lleva el perfume de bellos y heroicos dioses".

Quizás los héroes de hoy encuentren a los dioses si se atreven a escalar la roca del castillo de Brouzi o cuando visitan los monasterios y las iglesias de esta isla de 53 kilómetros cuadrados. Entre los turistas también son muy populares

a Corinto e in nove ad Atene (da Brindisi ad Atene sono in totale trentacinque ore)." La guida non dice però quanto tempo serve per arrivare a Brindisi da Colonia, Amburgo e Monaco.

Jannis Daskalos vive a Leros, una delle 3050 – più o meno – isole greche, di cui però solo 167 sono abitate. Di lavoro Jannis fa il pescatore, anche se le sue uscite in mare con la barca sono molto più frequenti l'inverno, quando la moglie trova il tempo per chiacchierare a lungo con le vicine. È molto più difficile pescare in estate quando sono tutti sempre impegnati per quasi venti ore al giorno. Allora Jannis fa il pescatore solo di tanto in tanto. Per la maggior parte del tempo si trasforma in proprietario di una pensione, va a far acquisti, serve ai tavoli e al bar. Da Maggio Eleni da casalinga diventa cuoca, lavandaia e donna delle pulizie, tiene i conti e riceve gli ospiti. L'arrivo dei turisti a Leros ha trasformato completamente la vita dei suoi abitanti. Di giorno gli stranieri provenienti dall'Inghilterra, dalla Germania, dall'Olanda o dalla Polonia rendono omaggio alle splendide spiagge e al mare, quel mare di una particolare tonalità di turchese così descritta nel 1932 dallo scrittore tedesco Kasimir Edschmid : „Il colore di questo mare è forse l'unica magia antica che il mondo ancora possiede. Nelle sue acque si sono rispecchiati tutti gli eventi della storia del nostro mondo. Questo mare ha visto sorgere e tramontare imperi con una tragicità e un colore noti soltanto al dramma mediterraneo. Basta solo sentirne l'odore: il profumo degli dei eternamente belli ed eroici."

Gli dei si rivelano ancora, forse, ai moderni eroi che scalano la roccia della fortezza di Brouzi o visitano i conven-

keinen freien Stuhl mehr. Griechischer Wein fließt in Strömen, Musik ertönt aus den Lautsprechern. Immer wieder dieselbe Melodie mit Bouzouki, Synthesizer und Percussion. Immer wieder Sirtaki. Die Fremden lieben ihn. Alle Welt hält den Sirtaki, den Alexis Sorbas im Film tanzt, für einen echten griechischen Volkstanz. Dabei ist der Sirtaki aus der Not geboren. Denn Anthony Quinn, der Sorbas-Darsteller, hatte so große Schwierigkeiten mit den griechischen Tanzschritten, dass man lieber gleich einen neuen, einfachen Tanz für ihn erfand: den Sirtaki. Dafür wühlte sich Mikis Theodorakis, der Komponist und Choreograf, durch den Fundus griechischer Volkstänze und Volksmusik. Die Tanzschritte sind vom Chassapikos, einem Tanz der Metzger aus dem alten Konstantinopel entliehen. Von einem Reigentanz, dem Sirtos, stammt der Name Sirtaki ab.

Nach Anthony Quinn, der mit seinem Alexis Sorbas Griechenland in der Welt populär machte, wurde auf Rhodos eine Bucht benannt. Ausflugsboote bringen die Touristen dorthin. Ob sie auch den Eindruck haben, den Kasimir Edschmid schilderte? „Alles hier war einfach – war nur Farbe, nur Linie, nur Licht. Es war das Diskreteste, was sich ein Mensch vorstellen kann in blassem Rosa, in schwachem Gelb und in leichtem Grün. Aber dahinter stand stets das dunkle, das Herz aufwühlende Blau des Ägäischen Meers." Oh, dieses Meer! Oh, dieses Licht!

Greek", is a genuine Greek folk-dance. But the sirtaki was born out of need, because Anthony Quinn, who played Zorba, had such difficulties with the Greek dance steps that a new, relatively simple dance was invented for him: the sirtaki. To this end, the composer and choreographer Mikis Theodorakis rummaged through the fund of Greek folk-dances and folk-music. The dance steps are borrowed from the 'hasapiko', a butchers' dance from ancient Constantinople. The name sirtaki comes from 'sirtos', a common name for a group of traditional Cretan dances in which the dancers form lines or circles.

On Rhodes, a bay has been named after Anthony Quinn, who made Greece popular throughout the world with the character Alexis Zorba, where excursion boats now take the tourists. Do they get the same impression as described by Kasimir Edschmid? "Everything here was simple – just colour, just line, just light. It was the most discrete that one could imagine in pale pink, in pale yellow and in light green. But always set against the rich, heart-stirring blue of the Aegean Sea. "Oh, this sea! Oh, this light!

« Zorba le Grec », est une véritable danse populaire grecque et pourtant le sirtaki a dû être inventé pour les besoins de la production. En effet, Anthony Quinn, Zorba le Grec à l'écran, n'arrivant pas à maîtriser les pas de danse grecs, il a fallu inventer pour lui une nouvelle danse toute simple : le sirtaki. Mikis Theodorakis, compositeur et chorégraphe, fouille alors le répertoire des danses populaires et de la musique grecque. Les pas sont empruntés à une danse des bouchers de l'ancienne Constantinople, le chassapikos, tandis que le nom sirtaki vient d'une ronde, le sirtos.

Une baie à Rhodes a reçu le nom d'Anthony Quinn qui, avec son personnage d'Alexis Zorba, a contribué à populariser la Grèce dans le monde entier. Des bateaux d'excursion y amènent les touristes. Ressentent-ils la même chose que Kasimir Edschmid à leur arrivée ? « Tout était simple ici – tout n'était que couleur, ligne et lumière. C'était la chose la plus discrète que l'on pouvait s'imaginer en rose pâle, doux jaune et vert léger. Mais avec derrière, toujours, le bleu sombre de la Mer Egée qui chamboule le cœur. » Cette mer ! Cette lumière !

las excursiones en ciclomotor para conocer la isla. En las suaves noches estivales resulta difícil encontrar una silla libre en las tabernas de Agia Marina o Platanos. El vino griego fluye a borbotones mientras suena la música de los altavoces. Casi siempre se trata de la misma melodía de Bouzouki, sintetizador y percusión. Y siempre se repite el Sirtaki. A los forasteros les encanta. Todo el mundo piensa que el Sirtaki que baila Alexis Sorbas en la película es una auténtica danza tradicional griega. Pero el Sirtaki es sólo el producto de una improvisación. En realidad Anthony Quinn, el autor que dio vida a Sorbas en la película, tenía tantas dificultades para aprender los pasos de las danzas griegas que se hizo necesario inventar una danza nueva y más simple para él: el Sirtaki. A este fin el compositor y coreógrafo Mikis Theodorakis registró el amplio fondo de las danzas y músicas populares griegas. Los pasos de la danza provienen del Chassapikos, una danza de los carniceros de la antigua Constantinopla. El nombre del Sirtaki proviene de una danza en corro, el Sirtos.

En la isla de Rodas se le puso a una bahía de nombre Anthony Quinn en agradecimiento al actor que, con su interpretación de Alexis Sorbas, había hecho popular a Grecia en el mundo. Los barcos de recreo llevan a los turistas a esa bahía. ¿Tendrán también los turistas la impresión que le inspiró este mar a Kasimir Edschmid? "Todo aquí era sencillo: sólo un color, sólo una línea, sólo luz. Ero lo más discreto que alguien se pueda imaginar en un pálido rosa, en un débil amarillo o en un ligero color verde. Pero detrás estaba siempre el oscuro, el conmovedor azul del Mar Egeo". ¡Oh, ese mar! ¡Esa luz!

ti e le chiese sparse lungo i 53 chilometri quadrati dell'isola. Un apprezzato modo per conoscere l'isola è girarla in motorino. Nelle miti notti estive non si trovano sedie libere nelle taverne di Agia Marina o Platanos. Il vino greco scorre a fiumi e la musica rimbomba dagli altoparlanti. Sempre la stressa melodia eseguita dal bouzouki, dal sintetizzatore e dalle percussioni, sempre il sirtaki. Agli stranieri piace e in tutto il mondo quello ballato da Alexis Zorba nel film è riconosciuto come una vera danza popolare greca. Eppure il sirtaki è nato per una mera necessità: Anthony Quinn, l'interprete di Zorba, era così impacciato nell'imparare i passi della danza greca che si preferì inventare una danza a sua misura: il sirtaki per la quale Mikis Theodorakis, compositore e coreografo, attinse al patrimonio delle danze e della musica popolare greca. I passi della danza sono derivati dal Chassapikos, il ballo dei macellai mutuato dall'antica tradizione di Costantinopoli. Da una danza condotta in circolo, il sirtos, deriva il nome sirtaki.

Ad Anthony Quinn, che con il suo Alexis Zorba fece conoscere la Grecia al mondo, a Rodi è stata dedicata una baia a cui attraccano i traghetti dei turisti. Che anche loro vedano oggi quello che scrisse Edschmid ? „Tutto era semplice qui – colore puro, linee pure, luce pura. Quanto di più delicato si potesse immaginare in quel rosa pallido, nel tenue giallo e in un verde tenerissimo. Dietro a questa visione, però, s'imponeva sempre l'azzurro penetrante e sconvolgente del Mar Egeo." Oh, quel mare! Oh, quella luce!

1	Vourvourou, Sithonia, Chalkidiki
2	Agia Trias, Thermaic Gulf, Chalkidiki
3	Nea Roda, Chalkidiki
4	Panteleimonos Monastery, Mount Athos, Chalkidiki
5	Megisti Lavra Monastery, Mount Athos, Chalkidiki
6	Simonos Petra Monastery, Mount Athos, Chalkidiki
7	Arnea, Chalkidiki
8 | 9 | 10	Monasteries of Meteora, Kalambaka
11	Mesolongi, Southwest Greece
12	Cape Leucadia, Lefkas
13	Tholos Temple, Delphi, Parnassos
14	Galaxidion, Bay of Itea
15	Brauron, Vavrona, Attica
16	Piraeus, Athens
17	Acropolis, Parthenon, Athens
18	Plaka, Lykabettos Hill, Athens
19	Temple of Poseidon, Cape Sounion, Attica
20 | 21	Thera, Santorini, Cyclades
22	Oia, Santorini, Cyclades
23	Nea Kameni, Santorini, Cyclades
24 | 25 | 26 | 27	Oia, Santorini, Cyclades
28	North Beach, Myconos, Cyclades
29	North Coast, Myconos, Cyclades
30	Venice, Myconos, Cyclades
31 | 32	City, Myconos, Cyclades
33	Terrace of the Lions, Delos, Cyclades
34	Paros, Cyclades
35	Temple of Apollon, Corinth, Peloponnese
36	Column Fragment, Corinth, Peloponnese
37	Mycenae, Kings' Graves, Peloponnese
38 | 39	Arcadia, Peloponnese
40	Monemvassia, Peloponnese
41	Gythion, Peloponnese
42	Vathia, Mani Peninsula, Peloponnese
43	Bourtzi, Methoni's Castle, Peloponnese
44	Platiana, Mount Minthi, Peloponnese
45	Olympia, Peloponnese
46	Venetian Castle, Heraklion, Crete
47	Knossos, Crete
48	Preveli, South Coast, Crete
49	Agios Nikolaos, Northeast Coast, Crete
50	Matala, South Coast, Crete

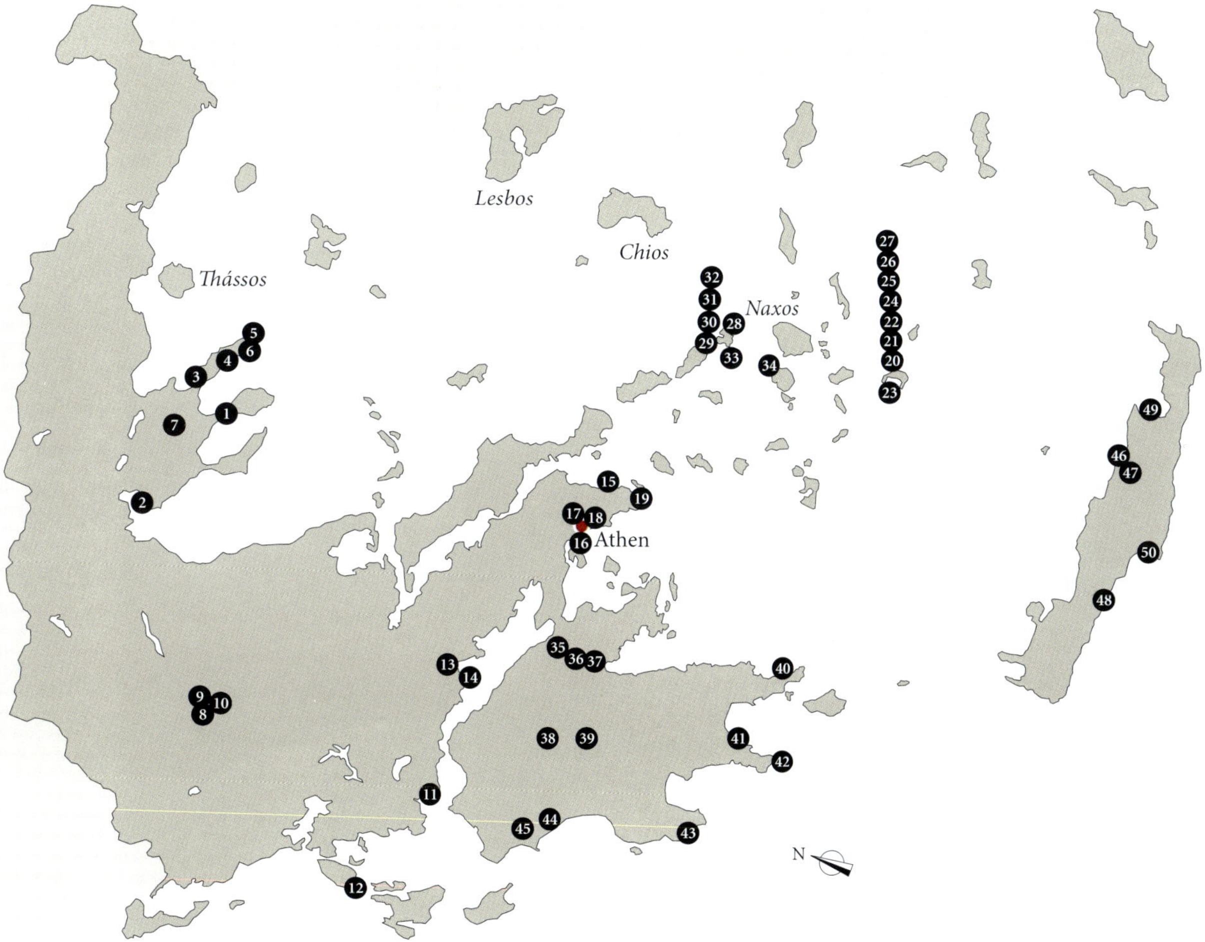

Lesbos
Chios
Thássos
Naxos
Athen
N
1
2
3
4
5
6
7
8
9
10
11
12
13
14
15
16
17
18
19
20
21
22
23
24
25
26
27
28
29
30
31
32
33
34
35
36
37
38
39
40
41
42
43
44
45
46
47
48
49
50

1 Vourvourou, Sithonia, Chalkidiki

2 Agia Trias, Thermaic Gulf, Chalkidiki

► 3 Nea Roda, Chalkidiki

ΝΙΚΟΛΑΟΣ Μ ΛΘ 11765

4 Panteleimonos Monastery, Mount Athos, Chalkidiki

5 Megisti Lavra Monastery, Mount Athos, Chalkidiki

► 6 Simonos Petra Monastery, Mount Athos, Chalkidiki

7 Arnea, Chalkidiki

 Monasteries of Meteora, Kalambaka

► 9 Monasteries of Meteora, Kalambaka

 Monasteries of Meteora, Kalambaka

11 Mesolongi, Southwest Greece

12 Cape Leucadia, Lefkas

13 Tholos Temple, Delphi, Parnassos

14 Galaxidion, Bay of Itea

► 15 Brauron, Vavrona, Attica

16 Piraeus, Athens

BARBIE-D

17 Acropolis, Parthenon, Athens

18 Plaka, Lykabettos Hill, Athens

19 Temple of Poseidon, Cape Sounion, Attica

► **20** Thera, Santorini, Cyclades

21 Thera, Santorini, Cyclades

22 Oia, Santorini, Cyclades

23 Nea Kameni, Santorini, Cyclades

24 Oia, Santorini, Cyclades

25 Oia, Santorini, Cyclades

► **26** Oia, Santorini, Cyclades

27 Oia, Santorini, Cyclades

► **28** North Beach, Myconos, Cyclades

29 North Coast, Myconos, Cyclades

30 Venice, Myconos, Cyclades

► **31** City, Myconos, Cyclades

MUSEUM
ΩΡΕΣ ΕΠΙΣΚΕΨΕΩΣ

 City, Myconos, Cyclades

► 33 Terrace of the Lions, Delos, Cyclades

34 Paros, Cyclades

35 Temple of Apollon, Corinth, Peloponnese

36 Column Fragment, Corinth, Peloponnese

► 37 Mycenae, Kings' Graves, Peloponnese

 Arcadia, Peloponnese

39 Arcadia, Peloponnese

40 Monemvassia, Peloponnese

41 Gythion, Peloponnese

▸ **42** Vathia, Mani Peninsula, Peloponnese

43 Bourtzi, Methoni's Castle, Peloponnese

44 Platiana, Mount Minthi, Peloponnese

► **45** Olympia, Peloponnese

46 Venetian Castle, Heraklion, Crete

► **47** Knossos, Crete

 Preveli, South Coast, Crete

49 Agios Nikolaos, Northeast Coast, Crete

► **50** Matala, South Coast, Crete

AXEL M. MOSLER wurde 1953 in Dortmund geboren, wo er auch sein Fachhochschulstudium der Photographie absolvierte. Seit 1977 ist er als freier Photo-Designer und Landschaftsphotograph tätig. Panoramaphotographie ist fester Bestandteil seiner photographischen Arbeit, die nicht nur in zahlreichen Bildbänden renommierter Verlage vorliegt, sondern auch auf vielen Ausstellungen im In- und Ausland gezeigt wird. Ausgedehnte Photoreisen haben ihn unter anderem nach Schottland, Norwegen, Kanada, Griechenland und in die Toskana geführt.

IRIS LEMANCZYK wurde 1964 in Kirchheim/Teck bei Stuttgart geboren. Nach dem Studium der Germanistik und Geographie lockte immer wieder die Ferne. Sie reiste um die Welt, schnupperte eine Zeit lang Zirkusluft, lebte in Namibia und besuchte für ein paar Monate Australien und Neuseeland. Dazwischen arbeitete sie als Zeitungs-Redakteurin bei der „Südwest Presse“ in Ulm. Seit 1997 ist sie freiberuflich tätig, schreibt Kinder- und Jugendbücher sowie Sachbücher, verfasst Reiseberichte und ist als Dozentin für Kreatives Schreiben tätig.

AXEL M. MOSLER was born in 1953 in Dortmund, where he also graduated from his photographic studies at the technical high school. Since 1977 he has been active as a freelance photo-designer and landscape photographer. Panorama photography is a permanent feature of his photographic work which is not only available in many illustrated volumes from renowned publishers, but is also presented at many exhibitions at home and abroad. Extensive photographic expeditions have taken him to Scotland, Norway, Canada, Greece and Tuscany among others.

IRIS LEMANCZYK was born in 1964 in Kirchheim/Teck near Stuttgart. After studying German and geography, she gave way to the call of far-distant places. She travelled around the world, experienced the circus life for a time, lived in Namibia and spent several months in Australia and New Zealand. In between, she also learnt something more conventional: newspaper editing with the “Südwest Presse” in Ulm. Since 1997 she has worked as a freelancer, writing children’s books and non-fiction and compiling travel reports, and also works as a lecturer on creative writing.

AXEL M. MOSLER est né en 1953 à Dortmund, où il fait des études supérieures de photographie. Depuis 1977 il travaille comme photo-designer indépendant et photographe paysager. Les panoramas qu'il photographie régulièrement ne sont pas seulement présentés dans les nombreux livres de photographies d'éditeurs réputés mais aussi dans de nombreuses expositions nationales et internationales. Les longs voyages entrepris dans le cadre de son travail l'ont conduit entre autres en Ecosse, en Norvège, au Canada, en Grèce et en Toscane.

IRIS LEMANCZYK est née en 1964 à Kirchheim/Teck près de Stuttgart. Après des études de philologie allemande et de géographie, elle effectue régulièrement des voyages lointains. Elle voyage à travers le monde, séjourne pendant quelque temps dans un cirque, vit en Namibie et passe plusieurs mois en Australie et en Nouvelle-Zélande. Entre toutes ces occupations, elle trouve néanmoins le temps d'apprendre un métier sérieux : rédactrice journalistique au quotidien allemand « Südwest Presse » à Ulm. Depuis 1997, elle travaille comme rédactrice indépendante, écrit des livres destinés à l'enfance et à la jeunesse ainsi que des livres d'essai. Elle rédige également des comptes rendus de voyage et dispense des cours de création littéraire.

AXEL M. MOSLER nació en Dortmund en1953, donde también realizó sus estudios de fotografía en la Universidad de Ciencias Aplicadas. Desde 1977 trabaja como diseñador fotográfico libre y fotógrafo paisajístico. La fotografía panorámica es parte esencial de su trabajo. Estas imágenes no sólo pueden apreciarse en un gran número de volúmenes publicados por casas editoriales de prestigio, sino también en muchas exposiciones tanto del país como del extranjero. Largos y extensos viajes fotográficos lo han llevado, entre otros lugares, a Escocia, Noruega, Canadá, Grecia y la Toscana.

IRIS LEMANCZYK nació en 1964 en el pueblo de Kirchheim/Teck junto a Stuttgart (Alemania). Tras terminar su carrera de Filología Germánica y Geografía se dejó atraer cada vez más por el encanto de los destinos exóticos: viajó por el mundo, experimentó durante algún tiempo la vida en un circo, residió en Namibia y pasó algunos meses en Australia y Nueva Zelanda. Y entre todas esas ocupaciones todavía encontró tiempo para aprender un oficio serio: redactora de periódicos en la editorial alemana "Südwest Presse" de Ulm. Desde 1997 trabaja como redactora libre y escribe diversos libros: desde literatura infantil y juvenil a libros de texto. Además confecciona relatos de viaje e imparte seminarios de creación literaria.

AXEL M. MOSLER è nato nel 1953 a Dortmund, dove si è laureato in tecnica fotografica. Dal 1977 è attivo come designer fotografico e fotografo di paesaggi. La foto panoramica è parte essenziale del suo lavoro che, oltre ad essere pubblicato in numerosi libri di fotografia per rinomati editori, è stato esposto in molte mostre tenutesi in Germania e in altri paesi. I suoi articolati viaggi fotografici lo hanno condotto tra l'altro in Scozia, Norvegia, Canada, Grecia e Toscana.

IRIS LEMANCZYK è nata nel 1964 a Kirchheim/Teck vicino a Stoccarda. Dopo la laurea in Lingua e Letteratura Tedesca e in Geografia ha seguito la sua passione per i viaggi in paesi lontani. È stata in tutto il mondo, per un certo periodo ha respirato l'aria del circo, ha vissuto in Namibia e per qualche mese ha abitato in Australia e Nuova Zelanda. Tra un viaggio e l'altro si è dedicata alla più razionale attività di redattrice presso la Südwest Presse di Ulm. Dal 1997 lavora come libera professionista, scrive libri per bambini e ragazzi e testi di saggistica, redige reportage di viaggi ed insegna scrittura creativa.

ISBN: 978-3-89823-338-5

Concept: Bernhard Wipfler, Sebastian Wipfler, Marcus Bela Schmitt
Design: Designgruppe Fanz & Neumayer | Marcus Bela Schmitt & EDITION PANORAMA | Diana May
Editorial department: Dr. Michael Barchet, Wolfgang Roth
Translations: Global-Text Fachübersetzungen, Heidelberg | Mark Woolfe, Jocelyne Abarca, Dr. Maria Carasi, Sebastián González Mohíno
Printing: abcdruck GmbH, Heidelberg
Bookbinding: Josef Spinner Großbuchbinderei GmbH, Ottersweier
EDITION PANORAMA GmbH
G7, 14
D - 68159 Mannheim

www.editionpanorama.com

A production by EDITION**PANORAMA**